GATWICK
AIRPORT

GATWICK
AIRPORT

Gordon Bain

Airlife
England

Copyright © 1994 by Gordon Bain

First published in the UK in 1994
by Airlife Publishing Ltd.

British Library Cataloguing in Publication Data
A catalogue record for this book
is available from the British Library

ISBN 1 85310 468 X

Printed in Hong Kong by World Print Ltd.

Airlife Publishing Ltd.

101 Longden Road, Shrewsbury SY3 9EB, England

INTRODUCTION

Gatwick's first airfield licence was obtained on 1 August 1930. The first scheduled flight from Gatwick was to Paris on 17 May 1936 and the fare was £4-5s-0d (£4.25) which included 1st Class rail travel from Victoria. Gatwick, situated on the main London to Brighton railway line, was the world's first airport to have a rail link to its capital city.

The outbreak of World War II brought a halt to development and the airport was requisitioned by the military on 6 September 1939 and returned to civilian control in 1946.

With the expansion of civil flying it was seen that a second airport for the London area would be required and, on 30 July 1952, the Cabinet Home Affairs Committee approved proposals to develop Gatwick. In October 1954 a second white paper was published and this was followed by Gatwick's closure in 1956 to allow construction work to proceed. The 'new' Gatwick was opened by H.M. The Queen on 9 June 1958.

With the continuing development of the airfield and its facilities, Gatwick expects to be capable of handling thirty million passengers by the year 2000. In terms of international traffic, London's Gatwick Airport is one of the world's busiest airports (London's Heathrow is the busiest). In terms of traffic volume it can be described as one of the world's busiest single-runway airports.

In 1989 Gatwick's aircraft movements exceeded seven hundred per day – the bulk of which were between the hours of 0600-2300. A movement is a landing or a take-off. The hourly rate of movements is regularly around forty-two during the peak hours with forty-five to forty-six being not unusual. To maintain these figures day after day demands peak efficiency from all sections of the airport from check-in and baggage handling through customs and immigration, refuelling and servicing organisations (technical and catering) and Air Traffic Control. The efficient use of the runway and surrounding air space means that, as one aircraft turns off the runway at the end of its landing run, the next departure has already lined up for take-off with the next arrival only three to four miles from touchdown.

The world recession of the early 1990s saw Gatwick's traffic figures fall with the sad demise of airlines such as British Caledonian, Air Europe and then Dan Air which was almost a family institution at Gatwick. But, despite some politicians' claims to the contrary, recessions do not last forever and most enterprises emerge fitter. Strong new airlines have emerged at Gatwick and the traffic figures are climbing again. Forecasts say that Gatwick will very soon be back at 1989 traffic levels and that they will continue to climb.

Two groups of people deserve mention. Airfield Operations staff are always patrolling the airfield checking on essential maintenance, be it cracked concrete on a taxiway or just a broken light fitting. Should an aircraft burst a tyre on the runway a 'Leader' vehicle can be on the scene instantly to organise the clearance of the debris during a temporary halt in the proceedings. Similarly the Airport Fire Service has an exceptionally rapid response time to any incident.

In the year ending May 1993, Gatwick had 173,955 aircraft movements carrying 19,811,000 passengers.

These are just a few of the many, many cogs in the large, highly efficient aviation machine that is Gatwick Airport.

Below: Northwest Airlines flies Boeing 747s on its trans-Atlantic routes. The engines seen here are Pratt & Whitney JT9s.

Opposite: Northwest Airlines is a major American carrier based at Minneapolis, St Paul, Minnesota. Here, one of fifty-six Boeing 747s in the airline's fleet departs runway 08R bound for Boston.

Below: Although painted in the colours of Air France, this SAAB 340 is operated by Brit Air (a Brittany-based regional airline) in association with Air France. This is part of a growing trend with major carriers around the world where regional airlines are 'adopted' and their schedules are arranged to interline with the larger carrier. This benefits both airlines as passengers transfer from one to the other flying between world destinations and the provinces.

Opposite: Basking in winter sunshine a Delta Air Lines Lockheed L1011 Tristar is pushed back by Tug 32. The ground engineer stands ready to supervise the engine start and to warn the pilot of any problems he might see. He has a headset which is plugged into a socket in the aircraft's nosewheel bay to communicate with the crew. If all is well he will remove the undercarriage safety pin and give the pilot the 'thumbs up' to let him know that all vehicles and personnel are clear of the aircraft. The crew can then request taxi clearance from the A.T.C. Ground Controller.

Below: The distinctive colour scheme of an Air New Zealand Boeing 747.

Opposite: An Air New Zealand Boeing 747-400, all its ground support equipment removed, is ready for push back for Los Angeles some ten-and-a-half hours flying from Gatwick and the first leg on its return journey to Auckland.

Below: Air New Zealand flies regular schedules from Auckland to Gatwick via Los Angeles using Boeing 747-400 aircraft. This variant of Boeing's very successful Jumbo is easily recognised by the upturned winglets at the wing's tips. Power is provided by Rolls-Royce RB211 engines. These are among the most powerful and efficient engines flying today.

Opposite: RFG Regionalflug is part of an operation called Eurowings, a West German airline. Scheduled services are flown to Gatwick from various German cities using both ATR 42s and ATR 72s. This ATR 42 is being pushed back for a flight to Bremen.

Below: Air Europe Express was the regional arm of the parent Air Europe company, itself part of the ILG Group of companies. With the demise of ILG, the Air Europe Express operation was salvaged by some of the directors and reformed into City Flyer Express using Short 360s. Expansion of the fleet brought the ATR 42 into the operation and the airline now has three, providing services from Gatwick to Antwerp, Guernsey, Jersey, Rotterdam, Newcastle and Dublin. City Flyer Express routes are interlined with British Airways, providing benefits to both airlines.

Opposite: City Flyer Express is a Gatwick-based regional airline which uses four of these ATR 42s on short-range services.

Below: Ambassador Airlines started flying from Gatwick during the 1993 season using Boeing 757s.

Opposite: Shortly a tug will arrive and take this Ambassador Airlines Boeing 757 from the maintenance area to a Gate where it will be loaded and depart for some hot and sunny holiday spot.

Below: The fin logo on Excalibur's Airbus A320s confuses some people, but imagine the hilt of a sword (Excalibur, of course) and it becomes obvious.

Opposite: Based at East Midlands airport, Excalibur started operations on 1 May 1992 using Airbus A320s on charter flights to Mediterranean destinations.

Below: New to Monarch Airline's fleet for the 1993 season was the Airbus A320-200, seen here preparing for a flight with Gatwick's Control Tower overseeing events.

Opposite: Monarch Airline's fleet includes eight Boeing 757s powered by Rolls-Royce RB211-535 engines. Service experience with this airframe/engine combination has shown the 757 to be one of the most efficient of the modern airliners.

Below: Tug 37 prepares to push back a Monarch Airline's Airbus A300-600.

Opposite: Most of Gatwick's parking gates are serviced by hydrant refuelling with fuel being fed to the gate by underground pipelines. This lessens the need for many large fuel bowsers driving around the airfield with all their attendant dangers. Instead fuel companies such as Air BP use a truck-mounted fuel pump to transfer fuel from the hydrant to the aircraft.

Below: Automatic transit trains carry passengers from the South Terminal, with its British Rail station, to the Satellite and North Terminals. The North Terminal, being much the busier, is served by two three-carriage trains like this one passing over the old A23, London to Brighton road. Should you be visiting Gatwick, but not flying that day, it is quite all right to travel on this train for a grandstand view of the airport.

Opposite: A feature of Gatwick's North Terminal departure lounge is this conical, stainless steel, water sculpture marking the entrance to the departure gates. It is surrounded by a spiral pathway to ease the problems of the disabled.

Below: Aircraft can get quite untidy after a two-hour flight. As soon as the last passenger is off the aircraft the cleaners move in. They, too, have to be quick and efficient as turn-around times for an aircraft can be very short. Here a Meridiana DC-9 receives their attentions.

Opposite: Two of Britannia Airways' Boeing 757s await departure from runway 26L.

Below: Britannia Airways operates a mix of Boeing 737s, 757s and 767s. Here a 737-200 lifts off from runway 08R.

Opposite top: An Airbus A300 and an Air 2000 Boeing 757 vie for position on runway 26L.

Opposite bottom: Passengers board an Air 2000 Boeing 757 on a glorious Gatwick day bound for Las Palmas. Air 2000 was born in 1987 using two Boeing 757s but now has a fleet of fifteen of these exceptionally efficient aircraft alongside four Airbus A320s.

Below: Stockholm-Gatwick services are provided by Transwede. This company was formed in April 1985 using McDonnell Douglas MD-87 and MD-83 aircraft.

Opposite: Gear almost tucked away, a Transwede MD-83 climbs out from runway 26L on its return to Stockholm.

Below: Rotate speed reached, the nose gear of this Continental Airlines DC-10-30 has just lifted off. In a few more seconds the aircraft's wings will generate enough lift to heave 250 tonnes of metal and people into the air.

Opposite: Continental Airlines is based in Houston, Texas and flies both Boeing 747 and DC-10 types on various scheduled services to the U.S.A.

Below: ETOPS (or Extended-range, Twin-engined Operations) has revolutionised trans-Atlantic travel. Airlines are aware that people don't just want to fly to New York or Los Angeles or Toronto. So, rather than operate one large aircraft to a small number of destinations, many airlines now offer smaller (but still wide-body) Boeing 767 and Airbus A310 aircraft to a greater variety of destinations.

Canadian Airlines offers world-wide services using a variety of aircraft but currently offers the Boeing 767-300ER on its trans-Atlantic flights to Gatwick.

Opposite: A Canadian Airlines Boeing 767-300 is pushed back, framed by the tail of another of the airline's fleet.

Below: Lufthansa flies the Boeing 737 from various German cities to Gatwick.

Opposite: Carrying a slightly 'different' colour scheme is this Braathens S.A.F.E. Boeing 737. This aircraft's scheme was designed by Norwegian schoolchildren as a promotional idea. The aircraft has just arrived from Oslo.

Below: Based mainly at Gatwick's North Terminal, British Airways is one of Gatwick's largest operators. With the sad demise of Dan Air, BA inherited most of their scheduled routes and, with them, the Boeing 737-400 aircraft which flew those routes. One of these former Dan Air aircraft lifts off from runway 08R en route for Paris' Charles de Gaulle airport.

Opposite: British Airways is one of the world's largest operators of the Boeing 747. After their initial purchase, in the late '60s when their aircraft were powered by the Pratt & Whitney JT9D engines, British Airways switched powerplants to the Rolls-Royce RB211.

Below: The takeover of British Caledonian Airways, in 1988, by British Airways brought the DC-10 into the BA fleet. Flying routes exclusively from Gatwick, these aircraft still operate the old BCAL routes to Houston, Dallas and Atlanta.

Opposite: Jersey European Airways dates back to 1979 when it took over the routes of the defunct Intra Airways. The airline was taken over in 1983 by the Walker Group. At that time the fleet consisted of Short 360s and Fokker F-27s. During the spring of 1993 three BAe 146s were added to the fleet allowing new routes to be opened up, such as Gatwick – Belfast. The F-27s operate mainly to the Channel Islands.

Below: Power for the BAe 146 comes from four Avco Lycoming ALF502 engines. These small turbofan engines are extremely quiet, making the 146 a very neighbour-friendly aircraft around the airfields from which they fly.

Opposite: Jersey European introduced the BAe 146 to its fleet during 1993 for services to the Channel Islands and Belfast.

Below: Amsterdam–Gatwick routes are flown by Transavia, which is eighty percent owned by K.L.M. The company was founded in 1965 and currently operates Boeing 737-200/300 aircraft alongside Boeing 757s. Only the Boeing 737s operate to Gatwick.

Opposite: A Transavia Boeing 737-200 taxies out with the South Terminal as a backdrop.

Below: TEA-Basel is a Swiss-based charter operator providing occasional flights to Gatwick during the summer months.

Opposite: Should you be lucky enough to go to the Seychelles on holiday, the chances are that you will fly on this Air Seychelles Boeing 767-200ER.

Below: Happy passengers disembark from an Airtours MD-83 after their Mediterranean hols.

Opposite: Airtours International MD-83 departs runway 26L.

Below: Although based at Cardiff, Wales, Inter European Airlines flies many of its charters from Gatwick using Boeing 737s, 757s and Airbus A320s. This is a Boeing 737-400.

Opposite: Servicing is all important in maintaining the very high standards of safety we have come to expect in the airline industry. The auxiliary power unit (APU) is a small gas turbine engine in the tail of most jet aircraft, which provides power to run the electrical, hydraulic and air conditioning systems when the aircraft is on the ground with its main engines shut down. Just like a car engine, it requires regular maintenance to keep it in top condition.

Below: American Airlines' MD-11s commenced services to Gatwick in 1993.

Opposite: Another ETOPS-equipped airline at Gatwick is American Airlines using Boeing 767s. On their busier routes, to Dallas for example, the larger capacity of the MD-11 is required.

Below: Unloading an Emirates Airlines' Airbus A310-300 which has just arrived from Dubai and parked at the North Terminal.

Opposite: Dubai is the destination of this Emirates Airlines' Airbus A310-300.

Below: 'Positive rate of climb–gear up'. The winglets on the MD-11 improve the aerodynamic efficiency of the aircraft, allowing greater range or a larger passenger load for the same amount of fuel.

Opposite: An American Airlines MD-11 makes an impressive sight as it breaks ground on departure from Gatwick's runway 08R bound for Dallas.

Below: Even a Virgin Atlantic Boeing 747 is dwarfed by the height of Gatwick's SMVCR, or Stalk Mounted Visual Control Room. Standing 135 feet high, it gives the Ground and Air Controller a spectacular view of the airfield and the surrounding area to aid them in their control of part of the busiest airspace in the U.K., if not Europe.

Opposite: Three hundred tonnes of Boeing 747, passengers, fuel, baggage and airline meals, departs Gatwick's runway 26L bound for Florida. Richard Branson's Virgin Atlantic Airways operates eight Boeing 747s on routes around the world. Further expansion is planned with the arrival of Airbus 340s.

Below: EVA AIR started services to Gatwick, from Taipei, using Boeing 767s. Traffic has now grown to the point where they have introduced the Boeing 747-400.

Opposite: EVA AIR started services from its base in Taiwan on 1 July 1991 with two Boeing 767-300ERs. Operating via Vienna, flights to Gatwick commenced in April 1993.

Below: Philippine Airlines uses Boeing 747 aircraft on its services to Gatwick from Manila via Frankfurt.

Opposite: Much freight is carried in the holds of scheduled passenger flights, but there are still many aircraft devoted to carrying purely freight. Affretair is a cargo airline based in Zimbabwe and is seen regularly at Gatwick with two Douglas DC-8-55F aircraft.

Below: Harare–Gatwick is served by Air Zimbabwe using two Boeing 767s.

Opposite: Keeping the grass cut to the correct length is important at airfields. Too long and it can impede the safety services. Too short and it allows birds to settle, causing a danger to aircraft from birdstrikes.

Below: Looking like large, yellow Daleks is one of Gatwick's transmissometers. Situated at the touchdown, mid-point and the stop end of the runway's edge, they operate in pairs to provide information to air traffic controllers, and pilots, about the visibility in foggy conditions.

This visibility is known as the 'Instrument Runway Visual Range' or, more normally, the IRVR.

A light is shone from one to another. A computer knows how much light is being transmitted and it compares that with the amount received at the other 'Dalek' just a few yards away. During clear weather the values are identical, but during foggy conditions the water vapour in the air scatters some of the light. The computer calculates how much light is being scattered and presents the result as a visibility in metres.

Behind, a Virgin Boeing 747 taxies to the runway with no need to know any of this information on such a sunny day.

Opposite: It is not only the aircraft which need regular maintenance, as the airfield itself comes in for its fair share of wear and tear. 'Leader 5' provides escort and radio cover for one of the airfield electricians while he replaces a broken taxiway light fitting.

Below: Transwede MD-83, Virgin Boeing 737-400 and EVA AIR Boeing 747-400 jostle for space at the Satellite Terminal.

Opposite: Meridiana uses the DC-9-51 as well as the MD-82 and the BAe146. This one has just left Gate 16 at the South Terminal.

Below: It has only just parked and shut down its engines on Gate 16, but the airbridge is already in place, the ground power unit is plugged in and the THF catering truck has just pulled up to this Meridiana BAe 146 from Verona.

Opposite: Caught in a patch of sunlight, a Meridiana BAe 146 taxies in from Verona against a dark, foreboding sky.

Below: An Air UK Leisure Boeing 737 nears the 26L holding point for departure.

Opposite: Air UK Leisure took delivery of its Boeing 767s in the spring of 1993.

Below: An Airtours MD-83 approaches the 26L holding point at 'Alpha North'.

Opposite: The light fades as a Gatwick handling tug tows an Airtours MD-83 to the maintenance area for routine maintenance after a long day's flying. An I.E.A. Boeing 757 follows.

Below: A mixture of diverse airline logos depict the style of operation that is Gatwick Airport. Nearest is the Picasso-style fin of Viva Air, a Spanish charter operator, behind is Transwede, a Swedish scheduled airline and, for trans-Atlantic services, farthest away is Delta Air Lines Lockheed L1011 Tristar. Easing in from the left is a Monarch Airlines Airbus A320.

Opposite: British Airways uses the North Terminal for most of its services and the mix of aircraft can be quite impressive. Here can be seen Boeing 737 and 747s alongside DC-10s, providing both short and long haul services around the world.

Below: Inherited from British Caledonian, the DC-10s of British Airways are still doing sterling service. Despite early problems with the aircraft, greatly exaggerated by the popular press, the DC-10 has matured into an exceptionally good aircraft.

Opposite: British Airways has ten Airbus A320s in its fleet. They are based at Heathrow but, occasionally, visit Gatwick.

Below: Air Malta placed three Boeing 737-300s into service during 1993 to complement their Boeing 737-200s and Airbus A320s.

Bottom: A queue forms at the 26L holding point as an Air Malta Boeing 737 touches down on Gatwick's single, busy runway.

Opposite: Caledonian Airways is a wholly-owned subsidiary of British Airways and operates services previously flown by British Airtours and the charter side of British Caledonian. Equipment includes Boeing 757 and DC-10 as well as the former British Airtours Lockheed L1011 Tristar.

Below: City Flyer Express uses four ATR 42s.

Opposite: A City Flyer Express ATR 42 awaits the arrival of an Excalibur Airbus A320 before, itself, taking the runway for Jersey.

Below: Formerly known as Gibraltar Airways, GB Airways is a Gatwick-based airline flying scheduled routes to Gibraltar and North African destinations using four Boeing 737-200s.

Opposite: A GB Airways Boeing 737-200.

Below: USAir flies daily ETOPS services to Charlotte and Pittsburgh using Boeing 767s

Bottom: Shimmering in the heat haze from the General Electric CF-6 engines of a USAir Boeing 767, a Cathay Pacific Boeing 747-400 arrives at the 'Alpha South' holding point for 26L at the beginning of a non-stop flight to Hong Kong's Kai Tak airport.

Opposite: A USAir Boeing 767 climbs out and sets course for Pittsburgh.

Below: Air traffic controllers get a spectacular view of aircraft when they are on Taxiway 8, as it goes right past the base of the Control Tower. This Cathay Pacific Boeing 747-400 is almost too large for the camera even when fitted with a wide angle lens.

Opposite: Another airline using the MD-11 on routes to Gatwick is Garuda Indonesia. The registration letters under the wing, EI-CDI, shows that the aircraft is registered in Eire, and the aircraft is leased from the GPA leasing company.

Below: Brit Air operates SAAB 340s in the colours of Air France with whom they have an operating agreement.

Opposite: Many different types of cargo find their way to Gatwick. This particular Royal Jordanian Boeing 707 is off-loading pallets of grapes.

Below: Pure cargo flights operate to the cargo terminal, to the west of the North Terminal. Okada Air is a Nigerian airline using Boeing 707s.

Opposite: A Braathens S.A.F.E Boeing 737 climbs out for Oslo.

Below: The Union Flag is interpreted in different ways by airline logo stylists. Air UK Leisure and British Airways both have extensive routes out of Gatwick.

Opposite: Monarch Airlines' Airbus A320 at the satellite building. Access to the Satellite terminal is via one of Gatwick's automatic trains which run all day, connecting the Satellite and North terminals to the South terminal with its British Rail station.

Below: Under a glorious summer sky a Cyprus Airways Airbus A320 is serviced for its return flight to Larnaca.

Opposite: Gill Air is a small regional operator with its Short 360s sharing Gatwick's single runway with the international airline's Boeings and Airbuses.

Below: Monarch Airlines' Airbus A320.

Opposite: A close-up of this Monarch Airbus A320 shows detail of the starboard 'winglet' and engine.

Below: TWA Boeing 747s fly routes to the U.S.A.

Opposite: Loading for Atlanta, Georgia, Delta Air Lines uses mainly the Lockheed L1011 Tristar on its Gatwick services.

Below: In a few more seconds, the wheels will be fully retracted. In two or three minutes, speed will have built up to the point where flaps and slats can also be retracted and this British Airways DC-10-30 will be the fast, sleek airliner that it was designed to be, cruising the world's airways at close to the speed of sound.

Opposite: A close look at this British Airways Boeing 767 will reveal an American registration. The reason for this is that BA has an operating arrangement with USAir after BA bought a $300 million stake in the airline. This is actually a US aircraft in BA colours with a USAir crew in BA uniforms.
A DC-10-30 taxies behind.

Below: With the break-up of the Soviet Union, many states now have their own airlines. Air Ukraine International is one of many which are using Western equipment in preference to the 'home grown' Tupolevs, Ilyushins and Yakovlev types. The Boeing 737-400 is the type favoured by many and is seen here taxying-in from Kiev on its weekly schedule.

Opposite: With independence from the Soviet Union, the Baltic States were keen to set up their own airline operations to the West. Amongst other types, Lithuanian Airlines uses Yakovlev Yak-42s on the route from Vilnius to Gatwick.

Top right: There are nine categories to which an airfield can be licenced and Gatwick rates Category 9–the highest.

The terms of Gatwick's Licence require that the Airport Fire Service achieves a response time of two minutes and not exceeding three minutes to the ends of the runway. A minimum of 24,300 litres of water together with 1,430 litres of foam concentrate must be available, to be pumped at a minimum rate of 9,000 litres per minute. To achieve this minimum standard, Gatwick A.F.S. has eight appliances– One Nubian Major, three Meteors and four Javelins.

Pictured here is a Javelin Major Foam Tender able to carry 10,000 litres of water and 1,177 litres of foam concentrate, giving the appliance the ability to produce 45,400 litres of ready foam per minute. Each vehicle weighs thirty tons and can accelerate from 0–80 k.p.h. in thirty-five seconds powered by a 620 h.p. Detroit turbo-charged diesel engine. The Monitor on the roof of the cab can be controlled from the roof or, remotely, from inside the cab.

Bottom right: Unlike 'normal' fire services, Airport Fire Services do not get many opportunities to attend 'real' fires, such is the safety of modern air travel. So practice sessions on the fire training ground are essential to keep firemen current with fire fighting techniques.

One of the more spectacular devices on the A.F.S. fire ground is the fire screen. This is a large sheet of steel with pipes placed around it. Through holes in these pipes fuel is sprayed and ignited. The temperature rapidly exceeds 800 degrees Celcius. In this shot, the fire has been burning about five seconds and the firemen have just started to put it out. A few seconds later the fire is extinguished.

Opposite: Gatwick's Airport Fire Service is situated at the base of the Control Tower, mid-way along the runway where it has quick and easy access to any incident. Speaking personally, I can testify that their reaction is second to none.
A Caledonian Boeing 757 taxies by.

Below: an occasional visitor to Gatwick is this Air UK Fokker 1000 about to be pushed back from Stand 8.

Opposite: Air UK was formed in 1980 by the merger of Air Anglia, Air West and Air Wales. Though based at Stansted Airport, Essex, Air UK operates scheduled services from Gatwick to Glasgow and Edinburgh. Whilst an Air UK BAe 146 takes on another passenger load on Gate 9, a Virgin Atlantic Boeing 747 departs runway 08R.

Below: Virgin Airlines has a fleet of Boeing 747s, but it also has this Boeing 737-400 painted in its colours for flights to Athens.

Opposite: Each Virgin Atlantic Boeing 747 carries this delectable artwork on its nose.

Below: Workhorse of the world's short to medium haul airlines, is the Boeing 737. Here a British Airways -200 series lifts off from runway 26L.

Opposite: As part of its fleet expansion programme and its policy of bringing other airlines under the British Airways umbrella, B.A. has taken a financial stake in the operation of City Flyer Express and their aircraft are gradually being repainted in the B.A. livery, under the title British Airways Express. The schedules are timed to interline with B.A.'s other route networks to provide a better service for the travelling businessman and holidaymaker.

127

Top right: Looking east from the Supervisors' position in the Control Tower. In the foreground, Anne Jermey records the weather for transmission to pilots. In the centre of the room is the airfield lighting panel and a ground movement radar screen. As it is daylight with good visibility, the position is not manned but, when in use, the taxiways will light up with green centre-line lights to guide aircrew to their parking gates.

To the right, in the background, is the runway, or 'AIR', controller, Paul Baker. To his left is the ground movement controller.

Bottom right: Situated on the top of the Control Tower is a radar aerial. This is the Ground Movement Radar, or GMR, and it displays a picture of the airfield whilst scanning at 60rpm.

In this picture runway 08R is in use and a small queue of aircraft is taxying to the end of the runway. One aircraft can be seen just airborne. Outside the airfield boundary, the radar has picked out the fields and hedgerows.

This equipment is mainly for use at night and in poor visibility but, as it is switched on permanently, controllers can use it during the day to check the position of aircraft on the manoeuvring area.

Opposite: a British Airways Boeing 747 nears runway 26L.

Below: Fins from opposite sides of the world meet at Gatwick. In the foreground is Stockholm-based Transwede and, behind, is EVA AIR's Boeing 747-400 from Taiwan.

Opposite: Maintenance plays a large part in any airline's operation. European Airlines, a Belgian-based carrier, started flying charter routes out of Gatwick during the summer of 1993 and one of its fleet of Airbus A-300s is seen here with engine cowlings open at one of Gatwick's maintenance areas.

Below & Opposite: It is a sad fact of life that some airlines do go out of business for one reason or another. Many airlines have come and gone at Gatwick, but it is fair to say that some of the best remembered are British Caledonian, Air Europe and, of course, Dan Air. These three airlines played a major role in Gatwick's history and development. This book is, primarily, concerned with what Gatwick is now and what it is likely to be in the future, but I include these three photographs to remind us of lost members of Gatwick's family.

Below: Eager with anticipation of an adventure to come, passengers are silhouetted against a Virgin Atlantic Boeing 747, watching as it is readied for departure to Florida.